Consi a Church Career?

Discovering
God's Plan for Your Life

Philip Bickel and Curtis Deterding

CPH

SAINT LOUIS

Dedicated to the role models,
both lay people and church professionals,
who encouraged and supported us
to offer our abilities to the Lord of the harvest,
and to the one who sends workers into his harvest field.

Contents

Part 1
DIALOG

The authors of this booklet have counseled hundreds of youth and adults about their future vocations. With few exceptions, these people have been full of questions. Perhaps you have some too. If so, we hope you'll find Part 1 to be a nice, friendly chat with honest answers to some of your concerns. Use the questions at the end of each chapter to ponder the concepts in your own mind.

Part 2 catalogs the smorgasbord of church career opportunities available for your consideration. The Resource List in Appendix 1 will direct you to other useful helps. The book concludes with a listing of colleges and seminaries of The Lutheran Church—Missouri Synod.

We encourage doing two additional activities essential to considering a church career. First, be faithful in Bible reading, prayer, worship, and the reception of the Lord's Supper. The better you know the Lord, the more clearly you will recognize his will for your life. Second, share your career questions with others. Talk with your pastor or other church staff. Converse with relatives. Listen to the advice of mature Christians. Find others who are pondering a church career. Meet with them regularly to discuss the matter. Perhaps you can study this booklet together as a launching pad for eye-opening, heartfelt conversations.

Some terms need to be explained. *Ministry* is a proper term for all vocations performed for the good of people and God's glory. However, in this book, *ministry* will sometimes be used for professional church work. When speaking specifically about pastors, we use the term *pastoral ministry.* The term *church work* can refer to the efforts of both paid church staff and volunteers. To distinguish between the two, we describe paid church staff with adjectives such as *professional, full-time,* and *public.*

1
What Am I Going to Do with My Life?

As the bell rang for class to begin, Mr. Beauchamp wrote on the board "28,000." After waiting 60 seconds, he asked, "Would anyone like to hazard a guess at the significance of this number?" Several futile guesses later, he explained, "Twenty-eight thousand is the approximate number of days the average person will live on this earth. My question to you is this: How do you intend to invest *your* days?"

Throughout our lives we all wrestle with the issue of selecting a career. As children we spend hours pretending "When I grow up, I'm going to be ..." and the next day we change our minds. The game becomes more serious as we mature. Even as adults we are not exempt from the career hunt. In the U.S., people average 10 job changes and three entire career changes per lifetime. The process doesn't get any easier with practice.

The word *career* comes from an old French word for "street" or "road." As you navigate down the road of your life, the most useful resource you will find is God's Word. In this chapter we briefly consider what the Bible teaches about the Lord's plan for your life.

1. God created you. This is so obvious that you may have failed to relate it to your career search. King David observed, "You created my inmost being; you knit me together in my mother's womb" (Ps. 139:13). In the same manner, the Creator designed you with your unique mixture of abilities and interests to be used in work that serves others. Taking inventory of your strengths and abilities, like David, you can rejoice, "I praise you because I am fearfully and wonderfully made" (Ps. 139:14).

As you consider how to invest your 28,000 days, please realize that you are not searching for just that one, single occupation that alone can make you happy. Because the Lord has given you several abilities and interests, you will discover several career options that appeal to you. Our generous Lord offers a smorgasbord of opportunities.

2. God recreated you. Due to sin, human strengths and abilities are often devoted to our own selfish purposes. On the cross of Calvary, Christ paid the price to liberate you from the penalty and power of sin. Through the water and word of Baptism you received "the washing of rebirth and renewal by the Holy Spirit" (Titus 3:5).

All that you were and all your abilities perished in your Baptism. But you weren't left destitute! Like Lazarus or Dorcas rising from the dead, you have been brought back from death to life in Christ. Reborn in Baptism, you are free to offer your strengths and abilities to the Lord as tools for accomplishing his will in our broken world (Rom. 6:13).

3. All Christians already share the same career. In the rite of Baptism the congregation addresses the newly baptized person, "We receive you as a fellow member of the body of Christ, a child of the same heavenly Father, to work with us in his kingdom" (*LW,* p. 204). That final phrase declares that in Baptism all believers are called to the same work: to expand God's kingdom as the saving Gospel reaches more and more people. No matter what other occupations we may have, building God's kingdom is our shared career, the road that we travel together. Together we invest our 28,000 days in the kingdom of God.

4. All occupations that are not contrary to God's commands serve people and bring glory to the Lord. Thus all such occupations please God. During some eras of history, Christians mistakenly have assumed that certain careers (such as being a priest, monk, or nun) were more religious and God-pleasing than the mundane careers of life (such as being a homemaker, laborer, or merchant). At the time of

the Reformation, Martin Luther reaffirmed the biblical truth that God calls people into all kinds of work.

5. Church careers are worthy of your consideration. Although a church career will not place you on a pedestal of holiness and privilege, it is a golden opportunity to serve others as your Savior has served you. Regarding the pastoral ministry, the apostle Paul said, "If any one aspires to the office of bishop [pastor], he desires a noble task" (1 Tim. 3:1 RSV). The same can be said of other professional ministry positions in the church. They are noble tasks, services worth performing, profitable investments of one's 28,000 days here on earth.

We invite you to consider these noble tasks in the chapters ahead.

Consider This

1. How do you feel about having an average of 28,000 days to live? What gifts and talents do you have to invest? How have you spent your days thus far? How do you intend to invest your remaining days? Share your life investment plan with a fellow believer.

2. You already have an occupation, because through Baptism you have been called to work in God's kingdom. How do you feel about this career? What personal abilities and skills would you like to offer to the task of building and expanding God's kingdom?

3. Which occupations have you looked at already? Which new ones seem most appealing to you? Why? How can each occupation be a way of serving people and glorifying God?

4. On a scale of 1 to 10, how interested are you in a church career at this moment in time? How much do you know about such careers? What do you need to learn to inform your consideration of a church career?

2
How Do I Know If God Is Calling Me?

Pastor Martin meets once a month with two people in his church who are considering church careers: Tony as a pastor, Liz as a deaconess. At one of their regular meetings, Tony said to Pastor Martin, "I guess I'd go to seminary, if I only could be sure God is really calling me."

"Lots of people feel that way," observed the pastor. "How about you, Liz?"

"The decision sure would be easier if I could be certain of God's will, if I had a clear call," Liz answered.

Pastor Martin smiled at them both and then asked, "Tell me, just what do you mean when you say you would like a call from God?"

"Well," ventured Tony, "if God really wants me to be a pastor, why not send me a sign like Moses got? Y'know—talk to me from a burning bush."

Liz laughed, "I'd settle for just a still, small voice, if I knew for sure it was from God."

The Desire and the Call

The apostle Paul speaks of the desire to be involved in public ministry: "If anyone sets his heart on being an overseer, he desires a noble task" (1 Tim. 3:1). This chapter will deal with two basic concepts: (1) the *desire* for the ministry; and (2) the *call* to the ministry. Failure to understand the relationship between these two concepts can cause one's consideration of full-time ministry in the church to come to a standstill. This chapter will demonstrate how to make headway.

The Desire

The desire for the ministry is an inner compulsion that arises from the heart in response to the love of God that is ours through Jesus Christ. How strong is your desire to be in full-time Christian ministry? Do you care about and want to help people who are hurting? Do you desire to lead people outside the church to faith in Christ as their Savior? Do you desire to care for believers, instructing them in the Word of God, counseling those in need, comforting the bereaved, and encouraging and training all to trust and serve their Lord more faithfully? Above all, do you wish to be apprenticed to the Lord, serving under his instruction?

These are important questions, because they reveal if you indeed have the desire to devote your life to serving God and people. This desire is often the first step used by the Holy Spirit to guide someone into a ministry career. Contrary to public opinion, following God's will does not doom us to doing things we detest. Rather, the Bible promises, "Delight yourself in the LORD and he will give you the desires of your heart" (Ps. 37:4).

In everyday conversation the desire of the ministry is often referred to as "a call from God." Although the desire is indeed a sign of God's leading, it is not one and the same as a call to the ministry. A proper distinction between the two will help you avoid some pitfalls, which we shall discuss in a few moments.

The Call

Regarding the Old Testament priesthood, Hebrews 5:4 says, "No one takes this honor upon himself; he must be called by God, just as Aaron was." The Augsburg Confession of the Lutheran Church echoes this teaching in Article XIV: "It is taught among us that nobody should publicly teach or preach or administer the sacraments in the church without a regular call."

Can you think of some examples of God calling people to a special task? Perhaps these quickly spring to mind: Moses, Gideon, Samuel, Isaiah, Ezekiel, Mary, the 12 apostles, and Paul. From these examples, some might conclude that a call is God's direct appointment, often accompanied by some miraculous sign. If this were the sole definition of a call, then how many pastors, teachers, and other church workers of today have been called? While God still works miracles, nowhere in Scripture has he promised to perform a supernatural sign every time he directs someone into the public ministry. Instead, Scripture tells us about another kind of call, less direct but just as much from God. In Ephesus, the elders were *elected* by their churches. Yet Paul told them, "Keep watch over yourselves and all the flock of which *the Holy Spirit* has made you overseers" (Acts 20:28, emphasis added). God's call came through the people's vote—from God, but indirectly so.

To summarize, the Bible speaks of two procedures by which God calls people into ministry: direct and indirect. Either way, the call is still God's call. And certainly the latter method is to be most expected in the church today.

Pushiness and Passiveness

Why have we distinguished between the *desire* and the *call?* Because the two are often confused. On the one hand, the call to the ministry is objective and concrete, namely, a request from a group of Christians to serve among them. On the other hand, the desire for the ministry is a subjective, inner attraction and compulsion to share Christ's love with people. Both the call and the desire are from God, but they should not be equated, or else one of two faulty attitudes may result.

The first faulty attitude is pushiness. This occurs, for example, when Chuck mistakenly thinks his desire entitles him to push himself upon some congregation as their pastor. Or Chuck may think to himself, "Because I am called, there is no need for me to educate myself for the ministry." People like Chuck need to learn three things: (1) the desire and the call are not the same; (2) God has given the authority to call a pastor to the church, not to the individual; and (3) the church has a right to set standards of training that must be met before someone may be entrusted with the office of the ministry (1 Tim. 3:9-10; 2 Tim. 2:2) or any church career positions.

The second faulty attitude is passiveness. This error occurs when someone says, "I am interested in the ministry, but I am waiting for God to call me. When he does, then I'll prepare for the ministry." This was the opinion expressed by Tony and Liz at the beginning of this chapter. On the surface this view may sound logical and humble, yet see what happens when the same reasoning is applied to another vocation.

Imagine a high schooler saying, "*After* an NFL team drafts me, I'll learn to play football." This example reveals a basic error of passiveness. To expect a call to the ministry before one has adequately prepared for that position is simply premature; it is looking too far into the future. It is counting one's eggs before the hen has even been hatched.

Proceed with Caution

The concepts of *desire* and *call* can be compared to a traffic signal. A green light represents the call. It flashes on when a church calls someone into a position for which he or she is trained and qualified. A red light represents no call. It flashes on either when the church does not recognize someone as qualified or when God gives someone a desire for a career outside the church. The red light may very well be God's open door to a vocation where a person can be a witness for Christ in the working world—a right turn on red, if you will.

There is one other color on a traffic signal—yellow—and it should not be overlooked. Flashing yellow means proceed with caution. The desire for the ministry is the yellow light on the traffic signal of God's will. If the light is flashing yellow, then you can and should proceed by aspiring to the ministry. "If any one aspires to the office of bishop [pastor], he desires a noble task" (1 Tim. 3:1 RSV). The Greek word that is translated as "aspire" means "to stretch out for." If God has given you a desire for a ministry career in the church, then stretch out for it, train for it, diligently work and plan for it. The response to the desire should be the positive action of aspiring.

Aspiring and proceeding with caution are not onetime activities. As you prepare for a ministry position, you will encounter many mini-decisions about what to do with your life: what to get involved in at your home church, what schools to attend, what kind of summer job to get. You can face these mini-decisions with confidence, because the Lord will be guiding you through them all.

To grasp this concept, picture the years before you as a highway that has several intersections with traffic signals. Traveling mile by mile down the road of your life, you will often come to a crossroads where the light may be red, yellow, or green. As long as the lights are flashing yellow, you can keep heading toward your destination of a church career, doing so with caution, but also with confidence that you are acting within the will of God.

The purpose of the rest of this book is to help you determine if you do indeed have such a desire and, if you do, how to aspire toward fulfilling it.

Consider This

1. In your own words define the *desire* for ministry. To what degree do you have such a desire? What church careers in particular are appealing to you?

2. In your own words define the *call* to ministry. What major steps still remain for you to become qualified enough for a church to extend a call to you?

3. Into which (if either) of the two pitfalls would you be more likely to fall: pushiness or passiveness?

4. Assuming God has given you the desire for the ministry, what can you do tomorrow to proceed with caution (the flashing yellow)? What can you be doing one year from now?

3
Do I Desire a Church Career for the Right Reasons?

With his learner's permit safely in his wallet, Norm was practicing parallel parking under the guidance of his father. As Norm backed in, the rear tire jumped the curb. "See? I did it all wrong," he complained.

"No," Dad corrected calmly, "you didn't do it *all* wrong. You only did one thing wrong."

"What's that?"

"Pull out and try it again, but this time position yourself one foot closer to the car in front of the empty space. If you start right, everything else comes easily."

That wisdom applies in many areas of life, including career selection. Some people, however, seek a professional church career for faulty reasons. The results can be frustrating and ineffective. In order to help start off your career search correctly, consider some of the improper reasons for desiring a church career.

The Social "Savior"

When I (Phil) was in college, I met Ron, who intended to enroll in a seminary after graduation, even though he did not believe in God. I could not help asking why.

He answered, "As a pastor I expect to make a significant impact on racial prejudice, poverty, and justice."

As worthy as these concerns are for the church, I hope the Holy Spirit got through to Ron at some point—or that Ron changed his career choice. If not, he would have become a threat to the faith of his parishioners.

To examine the genuineness of your faith, meditate for a couple moments on the following questions:

1. Do you believe in God the Father, Son, and Holy Spirit? (Mark 1:10–11; Eph. 1:3, 13)
2. Do you believe that you are a sinner who deserves nothing but separation from God eternally in hell? (Rom. 3:20, 23; 6:23)
3. Do you believe that Christ died for all your sins and rose from the dead? (Col. 1:18–23)
4. Are you absolutely sure that if you were to die today, you would go to heaven? (John 5:24; Rom. 5:1–2)

Can you answer all these questions with a confident yes? If you can, you apparently are building on the only proper foundation, Jesus Christ.

While we are on the subject of beliefs, some church workers experience a degree of unfruitfulness and frustration due to a faulty understanding of how God works to accomplish godly, fruitful living. Consider these questions:

1. Do you believe that God has made you new in Christ and empowered you for a life of service to him and to people? (Rom. 6:1–14; 2 Cor. 5:14–21; Titus 3:3–8)
2. Do you serve your Lord joyfully, out of thanks for his gracious pardon? (Eph. 2:8–10; Col. 2:6–7)

Only the Holy Spirit can recreate and equip you to live as God's child. If the concepts in these questions are unfamiliar, go to Scripture, your pastor, and other Christians to better understand and apply these truths that will help you serve the Lord with joy and fruitfulness.

Johnny One Note

It is possible for someone to be interested in church work simply because it will provide a chance to perform some favorite activity such as public speaking, administration, counseling, youth work, or social work. Such a church worker could be compared to the character in the light-hearted song "Poor Johnny One Note."

Where do you stand? The best way to learn is to spend time with persons in the career you are considering. Follow them through a typical day. Ask about the wide range of activities in which they are involved. Learn about the varied challenges they face. Then, ask yourself, "Am I honestly interested in a sizable portion of this ministry career, or am I attracted only to a small slice of it?"

To balance the picture, it should be added that church work affords many opportunities to specialize. According to the abilities and interests of the individual, he or she may become a specialist in counseling, evangelism, teaching, ministering cross-culturally, military chaplaincy, music, drama—the list goes on. Christian ministry opens the door to a variety of creative ways to serve the Lord.

The Heir Apparent

Some strong Christian families may assume that their children will grow up to pursue a church career as did Uncle Charlie the Pastor or Aunt Mary the Teacher. But when little Joey has grown up, he may realize that his desire for the ministry is simply a camouflaged ambition to please someone else.

Do you wonder about your motives in this regard? If so, do not feel guilty about it. Be thankful that you have Christian relatives and role models who have cared enough to encourage you to serve the Lord. Second, be honest with your family about all your career interests and ambitions. Third, most of all, be honest with God in prayer, so that you may know and do the will of your Father in heaven.

The Do-It-All

Church professionals have been uniquely trained for their work. Their job descriptions include responsibilities shared by no one else in the congregation. And they are good at what they do. Unfortunately, some situations encourage do-it-alls. The church staff feels compelled to take center stage and do all the ministry, and the congregation says, "We hired you to do these jobs in our place." Often the result is a worn-out staff and an immature laity.

To counteract this undesirable situation, the apostle Paul describes Christ's church as a body in which *all* the parts willingly serve according to the abilities God has given them. "We have different gifts, according to the grace given us. If a man's gift is prophesying, let him use it in proportion to his faith. If it is serving, let him serve; if it is teaching, let him teach; if it is encouraging, let him encourage; if it is contributing to the needs of others, let him give generously; if it is leadership, let him govern diligently; if it is showing mercy, let him do it cheerfully" (Rom. 12:6-8).

The professional church worker who teaches and encourages Christians to utilize their individual gifts will avoid the trap of being a do-it-all.

Proud Peacock

An inflated opinion of one's self can also affect ministry. The apostle Peter was well aware of this danger, for he warned the church leaders of his day: "Be shepherds of God's flock that is under your care, serving as overseers ... not greedy for money, but eager to serve; not lording it over those entrusted to you, but being examples to the flock" (1 Peter 5:2-3).

Public leaders always have been tempted by profit—emotional as well as financial. Human pride easily short-circuits effective ministry.

1. The lure of social status turns the work into serving self rather than God.
2. The substantial education of church workers can create a know-it-all servant of God—a contradiction in terms.
3. The praise of a job well done drives some to be more task-oriented than people-oriented, to ignore persons in need in favor of the mechanical aspects of the job.
4. Some conclude that working for the Lord makes them always right. The result can be unnecessary bickering and warring between believers. Meanwhile, the world looks on and says, "See how they hate one another"— the opposite of what Christ intended (John 13:34-35).

Nevertheless

Church workers are not faultless. Due to our sinful nature and the enormity of the work needed to be done in ministry, any and all of these temptations may prove irresistible at times. Nevertheless ...

All these transgressions were paid for by the Crucified One. When they are confessed, God's forgiveness is received and the Holy Spirit provides the sanctifying power necessary to keep pride from dominating in one's ministry. That's why Martin Luther cried out in a prayer regarding his role as a pastor,

> Lord God, You have placed me in Your church as an overseer and pastor. You know how unfit I am to administer this great and difficult office. Had I up to now been without help from You, I would have ruined everything long ago. Therefore I call on You. I gladly offer my mouth and heart to Your service. I want to teach people, and I myself want to continue to learn. Therefore I shall meditate diligently on Your Word. Use me, dear Lord, as Your instrument. Only do not forsake me; for if I were to continue alone, I would quickly ruin everything. Amen

Consider This

1. To what degree is your desire to serve the Lord a result of your faith in the Father, Son, and Holy Spirit?

2. Are you eager to do most of what a given church career entails? In order to pursue a career, how many of the responsibilities should appeal to you?

3. Do you have any family members or friends who would like you to prepare for a church career? Do you view their comments as encouragement or pressure? What can you do to communicate best with them?

4. Do you sense any possibility that you could become a do-it-all church worker? To what degree do you want to be the person who serves others? To what degree do you also want to be the person who trains and encourages others to serve?

5. In what ways might pride be playing a part in your desire to be in professional ministry? Compose a paraphrase of Luther's prayer, reflecting your own personal concerns regarding the church career you have in mind.

4
What Am I Afraid Of?

Amy, home from college for the summer, was talking with her parents about her career plans. "At school, I finally realized that God has a plan for my life. And can you believe I've read the whole Bible since last November?"

"That's wonderful, Amy," Dad said. "But why didn't you say anything during the year?"

Hanging her head a bit, Amy answered, "I wanted to tell you, but I was afraid, afraid because of something else that God was working in my heart at the same time."

"What's that?" inquired Mom.

"I'm thinking about some kind of church career. I'm pretty sure that's what I want to do."

"Praise the Lord!" Mom and Dad responded almost in unison. "But why were you afraid of that?"

"Because I knew you would be excited, and I don't want to disappoint you. I mean, what if I change my mind? Or what if I start and never finish? What if I'm a failure? Or what about my 101 other phobias? I don't know what to do. I'm stuck!"

Mom said, "I've got an idea. In April Pastor Kendall started a new group at church for people who are thinking about pursuing a church career. He has four or five people who attend. I'm sure that you would be welcome. And they'll help you get off dead center."

Some people get so bogged down in apprehensions that they never take a step forward toward a church career. Talk about your fears with a Christian whose opinion you value. And take time to talk to the Lord, too, because he who calms all fears can help you overcome yours.

The Fear of Not Finishing

We are taught from childhood that we should finish what we start, an ethic reinforced by a misinterpretation of Jesus' words in Luke 9:62: "No one who puts his hand to the plow and looks back is fit for service in the kingdom of God." Actually, Jesus is warning us that if we intend to be Christians, we must focus on him and not on the world. Thus, the verse is not a warning of spiritual disaster for anyone who drops out of a church vocation.

God indeed has a plan for all of his children, but professional church work is not on the blueprint for everyone. If after much prayer and soul-searching you decide not to continue aspiring to the ministry, fear not! God guides his children into careers of all kinds.

The Fear of Not Being Successful

Some assume that success in church work means serving a large church or preaching on television. This dangerous thinking will cause you either to abandon aspiring to the ministry now or to give up later when your ministry fails to be the booming success of your fantasies.

What does God say about success in his church? First, that *every* congregation, be it large or small, is the body of Christ. Second, that God gives differing talents and degrees of ability to his servants (Matt. 25:14–30). The Lord desires only that each of us be faithful in using what we have been given. Do not cater to the grandstand, because the world is not your audience. Seek to bring glory to God alone.

The Fear of Not Being the Type

Some people stereotype church workers (especially pastors) as living in a perpetual state of reverence. Certainly, church workers are concerned about spiritual matters, but they are a lively, humorous, fun-loving bunch with interests such as sports, gardening, music, cars, etc. Spend time getting to know the staff at your church, and you will see this for yourself.

Church workers are also pigeonholed as being "holier than thou," as separate from the real world. The reality is, church professionals often know a great deal about evil. They constantly touch the real world as they befriend and counsel drug addicts, adulterers, and the injured.

What type of personality does Jesus want? Trainable people who respond when he calls, "Come, follow me, and I will make you fishers of men" (Mark 1:17).

The Fear of Witnessing

The fear of evangelism is common, even among church workers. Therefore, every Christian has to learn how to share Christ—and how to overcome any fears associated with the responsibility.

If you find witnessing difficult, perhaps you need training and experience with an experienced person. I (Phil) can vouch for the process. I had a gargantuan dread of witnessing, but by going out on calls with others, the Spirit eventually provided the experience and self-confidence I needed to testify about our Lord.

Depend on the Spirit, who works through weak human beings like us. "God did not give us a spirit of timidity, but a spirit of power, of love and of self-discipline. So do not be ashamed to testify about our Lord" (2 Tim. 1:7–8).

The Fear of Being on a Pedestal

Church members tend to place professional church workers on a pedestal, expecting them to have a higher level of spirituality than other Christians. As a result, church workers sometimes feel like they live in a fishbowl, that their private lives are being held up to public scrutiny. They fear letting their hair down and being themselves in front of church members, and so do not develop friendships.

It does not have to be this way. The more you relate to people as a real person, the less likely they will be to see you as unapproachable. The more you are open and candid with people about your own struggles with temptation, the more likely they will be to see you as a fellow redeemed sinner. In that environment, friendships can grow.

Here are two other ideas for fostering friendships: (1) Spend time with other church workers and create opportunities to build friendships; (2) Join at least one organization outside of your church—Rotary Club, Toastmasters, a softball team, a hobby group, a civic committee, etc. Select a group that matches your interests and enjoy the friendships that develop.

The Fear of Ignorance of What the Job Entails

Because some people don't know the details of church work, they never follow through in their thinking about the ministry. Part 2 of this book will provide you some details about what specific church careers entail. To gain an even clearer perspective, talk with a church worker on the job—or, better yet, spend some work days with him or her, experiencing firsthand the aspects of that ministry.

The Fear of a Heavy Workload

Professional Christian ministries are very demanding. Studies of church workers reveal that they average 56 hours of work per week, with several spent in high-stress circumstances. Even when they are off duty, their minds may still be occupied with their occupation.

Although a church worker's schedule is full, it is also flexible, allowing opportunities for recreation or family activities. Many people who punch a time clock would welcome such freedom. And, in spite of the long hours, the reward of seeing people brought to peace with God makes it all worth the effort.

Finally, the servant of the Lord is free to take time off as needed, because his Lord never slumbers or sleeps. As Luther said, "While I drink my little glass of Wittenberg beer, the Gospel runs its course" (see Mark 4:26–29).

The Fear of Financial Problems

Finances can be a major roadblock for those who wish to pursue a career in the church. The costs of a higher education may seem out of reach. Where will the money come from to earn a college or seminary degree? There are at least three sources.

1. Self-employment. If you are a good student, a job of up to 20 hours a week should not hurt your grades. And some students take off a semester or year to earn money.

2. Scholarships and loans. College and seminary representatives can guide you to these sources of income, so that you can graduate with as small a debt as possible.

3. Employment of spouse. If the spouse who is not a student can work full time or part time, the family can often make ends meet.

Some people's financial fears focus beyond graduation. And true, only half the ministers in North America earn the median income. Put your fears to rest by putting stock in the Lord's financial counsel: Seek first my kingdom and my righteousness, and all these things will be given to you as well (adapted from Matt. 6:33). Honest financial planning sessions with the Lord will bring dividends that the world cannot give—contentment with what one has, and satisfaction from performing highly rewarding work.

The Fear of "Alligators"

Parish "alligators" have been found in every time and every clime. Long ago Moses had to deal with droves of them in the arid Sinai Peninsula. The apostle John describes a malicious gossiper (3 John 9–10). We all have faults and problems, but an alligator is someone with problems who makes himself a problem for the church.

How is one to deal with alligators? First, realize that alligators are the exception, not the rule. Some churches have none at all. Second, you do not face alligators one on one. You will have the support of other church staff, elders, neighboring pastors, and superiors within your denomination. Third, through troublemakers, God can discipline you to be more sensitive to confused, hurting people. And genuine, fruit-of-the-Spirit love can eventually turn an alligator into an alleluia.

The Fear of Not Being a Good Team Player

One year, the soccer team I (Curtis) coached had fantastic chemistry. Their strengths and weaknesses complemented each other. With no superstar (and, therefore, no "hot dog"), the players all knew that not one of them could coast or slack off; their total effort was always needed.

More than likely, you will never serve a congregation as the only professional worker. Few such congregations exist any more; and even where they do, the pastor plus the volunteers make up the team. The question is, what can you do as a part of that team, both now as a volunteer and later as a professional? Although the Holy Spirit calls a team together, you can learn to be a good team player by developing the elements of team chemistry.

1. Bond with the team. The more you respect, support, and encourage one another, the more smoothly you will work together. Bonding occurs on the deepest level when you pray and study the Word of God together.

2. Accept the strengths of others to compensate for your weaknesses. Team ministry allows you to specialize in your areas of strength and interest. And remember, when someone complements your weakness with their strength, be sure to compliment them for a job well done.

3. Good athletes know where the other players are, even when they cannot see them. Quality church teams often discuss their philosophies of ministry, their priorities and goals. They know where the others are at: what they are thinking, where they stand, and what their priorities are.

4. Give your total effort, for team members are accountable to one another. They give every assignment their best shot. And when they experience difficulty in completing a task, they inform their teammates about it as soon as possible, so that they all can seek solutions to the situation. Teammates are also accountable to each other in regard to rest. If someone is overdoing it and on the way to the emotional black hole of workaholism, teammates step in with warnings. That's being a professional.

5. Aim for servanthood, not superstardom. Jesus calls

professional church workers to live out a paradox: lead by serving. "Whoever wants to become great among you must be your servant, and whoever wants to be first must be slave of all" (Mark 10:43–44).

The Fear of Ridicule and Persecution

If you have stood up for what you believe, no doubt you have experienced ridicule. Some people have little respect for Christianity. Those in the church who cause scandal have damaged the reputation of the whole church. In addition, anti-Christian elements are on the rise in North America. It is no longer "in" to be a Christian. In spite of that, church workers generally are held in high regard by those in their congregations and communities who know them personally. The same will likely be true for you.

As long as we have opened this can of worms, let's be honest. It is possible that during your lifetime local anti-Christian opposition could boil to the point of open persecution. The apostle Paul did not hide this possibility from new converts. "We must go through many hardships to enter the kingdom of God" (Acts 14:22), he warned.

In recent centuries, Christians in the West have been relatively safe, but the 20th century has had more Christian martyrs than all the centuries before it put together. Martyrdom usually occurs where missionaries are breaking Satan's death grip. Paul did not see this prospect as a liability, but as simple reality, even an honor: "For it has been granted to you on behalf of Christ not only to believe on him, but also to suffer for him" (Phil. 1:29).

Your Lord urges you to take up your cross and follow him. "For whoever wants to save his life will lose it, but whoever loses his life for me and for the gospel will save it" (Mark 8:35). He never said it would be easy, but he did say it would be worth it.

Consider This

1. In your opinion, do the authors dwell too much on

the negatives of ministry? Or do you welcome honest discussion of these concerns? Explain your responses.

2. What are some reasons why it is hard for us to admit our fears to another Christian or to God?

3. Do you think any of the above fears are minor? With which fears have you wrestled? To what degree do the author's comments help you deal with your fears?

4. Think and pray about the apprehensions you have toward becoming a church worker. Are there issues of importance to you that were not mentioned here? Find someone with whom to share them.

5. Problems will arise in professional ministry; but when they do, you are not on your own. Talk to a professional church worker to discover the many resources available to help you.

5
Where Do I Begin? Will I Ever Be Ready?

Pat rapped on the door of Tim, the director of Christian outreach at St. Mark. "Got a minute, Tim? I want to talk about my dream of going into church work."

"Good," Tim encouraged. "I'm glad to hear you're still thinking about it. So, what's up?"

"Well, what do I do next? Where do I begin? Will it take forever? Will I ever be ready?"

"Sounds like you're feeling a bit overwhelmed."

"Yes! I'd like to move along quickly, but it seems like I have so far to go. I haven't even started college yet."

Tim reached for his Bible and opened it to 1 Timothy 3:1. "Listen to what Paul says here, 'If any one aspires to the office of bishop'—that means a pastor—'he desires a noble task' [RSV]. *Aspire* means 'to stretch out for.' So, Pat, when God gives you a desire for a ministry career in the church, then stretch out for it, be trained for it, diligently work and plan for it—even while you're still here at St. Mark. God has lessons to teach you before you head off to college. Do you think you can learn them?"

"Well, I guess I can try," Pat offered.

God has already started you aspiring by calling you to faith in Christ and leading you to serve in your church. You have continued the process by reading this book and, we hope, by discussing your desires with your pastor and other Christians. This chapter will provide further information about aspiring, namely, the qualifications for ministry; the training you can receive right where you are now; and the training you will receive through formal education.

Qualifications

In 1 Timothy 3:1–13 and Titus 1:5–9 Paul talks about the qualities that hinder the testimony of church workers and that enhance the receptivity of those to whom they minister.

Upright Behavior

Paul tells us that pastors and other church workers must be blameless, above reproach, upright, holy. They must have a good reputation with outsiders and love what is good. Paul, however, is not demanding unattainable perfection. He is throwing out a challenge. When we daily offer our sinful hearts to God to receive his Son's fresh cleansing, then by the Holy Spirit's power we are able to approach the standards set forth in these Scriptures.

Self-Control

Church workers need to master their natural desires and to be temperate, self-controlled, disciplined, and gentle. Likewise, there are negative qualities to be overcome: not given to drunkenness, not violent, quarrelsome, overbearing, or quick-tempered. North Americans today are prone also to several other negative behaviors often winked at or even applauded by some: workaholism, eating disorders, deficit spending, and perfectionism. Since it is easy to deny these weaknesses in ourselves, ask others for their evaluation. How might God help you to improve where needed?

Attitude toward Material Possessions

Those who work for the church should not be lovers of money. Christians can be overcome by worldly goods and activities without realizing it. No one is immune to this temptation. On the positive side, Paul insists that the pastor be hospitable. In the early church, Christians provided shelter and food to fellow believers who were widowed or orphaned or were fleeing from persecution or simply were traveling through town. Every generation provides church workers with ample opportunity for hospitality.

Ability to Teach

The job descriptions of most church workers include

teaching. Pastors are teaching at the same time they are preaching. The deaconess teaches while counseling a dysfunctional family. The director of Christian outreach teaches while taking church members along on evangelism calls. The director of parish music teaches while helping the choir to understand and appreciate the words of an anthem. In fact, a church worker rarely goes through a day without instructing people in some way.

Therefore it comes as no surprise that Paul advises Timothy to seek candidates who are "able to teach." This ability involves using and communicating sound doctrine in such an effective and personable manner that it is truly understood, believed, and acted upon. True teaching is not simply the communication of bare facts; it's helping people put the facts into practice. Having a Christian education is bearing the fruit that grows from hearing God's Word.

Family

Evidently, the church worker's family is of critical importance. Paul enjoins pastors to be "the husband of but one wife" (1 Tim. 3:2). His words merit repeating in our day, as immoral ideologies war against marriage and as even Christians seek divorces. The only Scriptural grounds for divorce are adultery (Matt. 19:3–9) and desertion (1 Cor. 7:15). Readers of this book who have been divorced ought to discuss this matter with their pastors.

The character of a church worker's spouse also merits scrutiny. Regarding wives of deacons, Paul says, "Their wives are to be women worthy of respect, not malicious talkers but temperate and trustworthy in everything" (1 Tim. 3:11; see also Prov. 31:10–31).

Likewise, Paul speaks of the pastor's relationship with his children: "He must manage his own family well and see that his children obey him with proper respect" (1 Tim. 3:4). "An elder must be ... a man whose children believe and are not open to the charge of being wild and disobedient" (Titus 1:6).

Clearly, Paul advises that those who serve the church

should demonstrate the sacredness, joy, and strength of a Christ-centered family.

Proven Spiritual Maturity

There is a saying in high school and college football that for every first-year player on the starting team, the coach should expect to lose one game. Since ministry in the church is of such critical and eternal consequence, Paul specifically warns against turning responsibility over to those who lack spiritual maturity: "He must not be a recent convert, or he may become conceited and fall under the same judgment as the devil" (1 Tim. 3:6).

Paul gives a helpful definition of spiritual maturity in 1 Timothy 4:12: "Set an example for the believers in speech, in life, in love, in faith and in purity." Such qualities are usually the result of a gradual process of spiritual growth over months or years. Paul speaks of the needed maturing process in 1 Timothy 3:10, "They must first be tested; and then if there is nothing against them, let them serve as deacons." The time of testing is carried out as you serve as a volunteer in your local church and as you study to prepare yourself for church work responsibilities.

Blessed Assurance

Even though aspiring to the professional ministry is serious business, here is important advice: Relax. Rest in the knowledge of God's never-ending love for you. God chooses weak people like us for his ministry purely on the basis of his mercy and grace. So take it easy on yourself. You do not have to be forever scrutinizing and evaluating your fitness for service in the church's ministry. Simply enjoy your activity in the church and your academic preparation. And give yourself and the Holy Spirit time for his fruit to mature on the vine of your life.

Training Now

The Training Center

In every congregation, God has gathered together a small segment of the entire holy Christian church. This communion of saints is a training center in which the Christian faith is shared and Christian living is dared. The congregation is the training center for all Christians, both those who wish to aspire to a professional ministry role and those whose goal is to become more dedicated lay people.

Strive to gain experience in different areas, perhaps even making a long-range plan. For example, a plan for a teenager or college student might look like this:

YEAR ONE	YEAR TWO	YEAR THREE
Worship	Worship	Worship/greeter
Bible class	Bible class	Bible class
Daily devotions	Daily devotions	Daily devotions
Youth activities	Youth activities	Youth activities
Evangelism training	Personal witnessing	Personal witnessing
Music/choir	Teach Sunday school	Shut-in visits
	Servant event	A mission trip

An adult's long-range plan might include stints as youth group counselor, evangelism caller, elder, trustee, Sunday school teacher, member of the church council, caregiver, small group Bible study leader, or any of the many other important areas of Christian service. Such on-the-job training is of immeasurable value. Those who find joy and fulfillment in these areas of ministry can consider assuming further responsibilities.

The Trainers

The head trainer is your local pastor. St. Paul informs us that the pastor's main objective is "to prepare God's people for works of service, so that the body of Christ may be built up" (Eph. 4:12). Allow your pastor to prepare you for works of service. Attend his classes, take notes on his sermons, learn from his example, and apply what you learn to your life. Seek his advice and that of other church workers.

Your pastor and local church staff are not your only trainers. You can learn from every member of the congregation. Where the people of God are working and growing together, they are encouraging and training one another. This is especially true in small group Bible study. In such a setting we can "consider how we may spur one another on toward love and good deeds" (Heb. 10:24). If your church doesn't offer such a group, talk to your pastor or other church staff person about starting one.

The Training Manual

The Bible is God's training manual. You will be properly equipped to serve the Lord to the degree that you are in regular contact with His Word. Sunday worship is the key method of growing in Scripture, and we have already mentioned the importance of small group Bible study.

To some extent, spiritual training is like lifting weights. For example, when you serve as a Sunday school teacher, you lift the weights of dealing with rowdy children, of making difficult concepts understandable to young minds, of helping each child to know Jesus as his or her personal Savior, of visiting the parents who do not permit their children to attend classes regularly. As you carry such weights with you into your devotional time, the barbell gets heavier, God's Word speaks to your needs, you wrestle in prayer (Col. 4:12), and spiritual muscles become firm.

If you have trouble establishing the habit of daily devotions, start small. The weight lifter who can bench-press 300 pounds began training with something less. Be content to start small. The Holy Spirit will work with you.

The Tools

Our God, in his grace and wisdom, has also equipped all Christians with tools to be used in serving him. We call these tools "gifts of the Holy Spirit." Every Christian has at least one, and many have more.

The Bible provides detailed instruction concerning the gifts of the Holy Spirit (see Romans 12, 1 Corinthians 12, and Eph. 4:1–16). Study these texts on your own. In each of these readings the church is compared to the human body—many parts with different functions, all necessary.

Depending on your spiritual gifts, natural talents, and the needs of your church, the possibilities will be thrilling to behold. If you do not know what your spiritual gifts are, ask your pastor or another church staff person to teach you how to discover and utilize them.

Future Training: Formal Education

Not everyone is thrilled when they consider the years of school that lie between them and their career goal as a professional church worker. The reluctance is often multiplied if one has already been out in the working world for some time. All the years of book cracking and term-paper writing may seem as vast, dry, and uncrossable as the Sahara. Some people wonder if it's really necessary.

A broad education will help you understand what is happening in the world and to communicate effectively with the people in it. Education will enhance your ability to create, to develop new ideas and strategies on your own initiative. In the case of a pastor, for example, a broad education will keep him from sounding like a broken record as he produces at least 2,700 sermons and teaches for at least 7,000 hours in a 40-year career.

A solid education is needed to help you answer the multitude of questions people have about religion. Quality education helps you to communicate with the unbelieving intellectual and to explain profound theological concepts in simple language to little children. Wide learning and experience are needed to successfully confront the cults and world religions that are gaining headway in North America.

Also, solid biblical education is needed to be a person who "correctly handles the word of truth" (2 Tim. 2:15). A church worker with a superficial knowledge of the Word is more likely to fail to make a proper distinction between Law and Gospel, with the result that the unrepentant will not be shown the full gravity of the Law or that the repentant believer will not be offered the Gospel in all its liberating sweetness.

The schooling is not a snap, but each school term you

will rejoice in what you have learned and gain more confidence for your career.

Areas of Study

Biblical studies. Obviously, someone who works in the church should be extremely familiar with the Bible—its books, history, characters, and teachings. You will need to correctly interpret and apply the Scriptures to questioning people in today's world. Seminaries require students to attain a working knowledge of the original biblical languages, Hebrew and Greek, which helps one avoid errors of interpretation and provides insights for teaching and applying God's Word to everyday life.

Church history. To know who you are, it helps to know where you came from. Christianity is not limited to one century or denomination. The study of church history provides a full picture of the body of Christ, how it has come to where it now stands and where it is headed.

Doctrine. All of Scripture is interesting, but our minds also appreciate arranging the Bible's teachings (doctrines) in logical, systematic patterns. A catechism is the most familiar example of this. Through study of doctrine you become thoroughly equipped to teach, rebuke, correct, and train others in righteous living (2 Tim. 3:16).

Practical theology. Nothing is more important to learn than "how-to." Courses in practical theology provide biblical direction and experience in preaching, teaching, evangelism, administration, worship, counseling, mission education, motivation for Christian giving and lifestyle, etc. These courses do not perfect the student, but by means of years of study, you will gain the ability to carry out basic ministry skills in a biblically sound manner.

Areas of specialization. Each church ministry academic program includes many courses in a specialized area—education, evangelism, cross-cultural ministry, music, etc. If you have more than one interest, you can take elective courses in other fields as you broaden your abilities.

More Facets of Education

In order to balance the picture, please realize that your formal education will be much more than reading and writing. In addition to the academic challenges, there is a sizable emphasis on practical, on-the-job training—some in connection with class work, plus up to a year of intensive training in a parish or a Christian agency.

While in school, spiritual growth is encouraged through daily chapel services, with messages delivered by faculty and students alike. Also, you will grow in the fear and knowledge of the Lord as you continue to spend time in group Bible study and private devotions.

Education also occurs through fellowship and friendships with professors, who often have years of experience in ministry. They add to the instruction the ingredients of their own personalities and interests. Eager to help students, their office doors usually are open.

Fellow students are the spice of campus life. The variety of students is refreshing. Your class may well include an accomplished musician, a physically challenged person, a student from overseas, a former Air Force officer, a woman who has raised a family, and someone with a background like yours. You will learn marvelous lessons from each one.

Conclusion

The process of aspiring toward a church vocation can result in a red light (as discussed in chap. 2). Remember, though, you can turn right on red. To have tried is better than to have never taken a shot at your goal. To have experimented and concluded you would rather do something else is the Lord's guiding. Whichever way he leads you, he intends to bless you in your occupation. What you have learned in the local church or in school will not be wasted. You will surely put it to use often in your daily life.

If your preparation concludes with a green light (a call to serve in a professional ministry), you will be sure of two things. First, the Lord has guided and strengthened you all along the way. How you will praise him! Second, you will know that God is not finished with you yet, because you will have been prepared for only an entry-level position in the church. As God's apprentice, you will always be learning and depending on him; and as the Master, he is ready, willing, and eager to teach you.

Consider This

1. How well do you fit the qualifications for ministry in the church? Seek the opinion of your pastor and other mature Christians. The Holy Spirit often guides through the caring counsel of other believers.

2. Picture your church as a training center. In which activities would you benefit from participation? Who are the trainers with whom you should interact? What are ways you can get a better grasp of the training manual, the Bible? Chart a multiyear plan of how in your local church you can develop ministry skills and a servant attitude.

3. What questions do you have about the formal education necessary for you to become prepared and qualified for a call? What people or schools can help you answer your questions? Discuss your questions with any students who are presently studying for a church career.

4. On the basis of the information in this chapter, how do you feel about aspiring toward a church career? Are you encouraged or discouraged, confident or bewildered? Share your reactions with others.

6
Where in the World Will God Send Me?

Laura was 17 and trying to decide on a college. Brian was a Vietnam War vet, married with four kids, and wondering whether he could tolerate still being a salesperson. At one of their church's career meetings, Laura confessed, "I guess what bothers me most is, God could send me anywhere. It's kind of scary. I could wind up alone in some distant city a thousand miles from my family and friends."

Brian chuckled, "I've had nightmares like that myself." He paused a moment and then reread the topic question: *Where in the world will God send me?* "Uh oh. It says, 'Where in the *world* ...' World could mean Africa, Latin America, Asia—maybe even Vietnam."

"Or," responded Laura, "'world' could include inner-city North America, or deaf ministry ..."

"Or prison ministry," Brian interrupted.

"Or retarded children."

"Or street gangs."

"Or AIDS victims."

"We sure have enough *ors* in the water," Brian joked.

Laura nodded in agreement, but her face expressed more apprehension than confidence. "Putting your future in God's hands, in the church's hands, is a real step of faith."

Call Procedures: The Green Light

By means of the church's call, God will send you to the place where he wants you to serve. The procedure varies among denominations. In some, vacant congregations interview and then vote whether to extend a call to a candidate.

If they vote yes, then the candidate must decide whether or not to accept the call. In other denominations, a placement committee composed of church leaders assigns graduates to those congregations that have a vacant position. The committee, of course, strives to place people where they will be most effective and content. In both models, the Holy Spirit works through the people involved to accomplish his holy will and place his workers in the section of the harvest field where he needs them (Matt. 9:38; Acts 20:28).

Can God Be Trusted with My Future?

Many people considering a career in church work have wondered, "What if I am sent someplace where my skills are not utilized or my efforts are not appreciated? If that happens, will the long years of study have been worth it?" Ultimately, the question is this: Does God really call through the decision of the church; and, if so, can God be trusted to choose what is best for me? I (Phil) know he can and does.

In my second year at seminary, I longed to do campus ministry. Recalling the uncertainty of my own college days, I wanted to provide direction for other young people who were drifting in life without a clear course to sail. There was just one minor obstacle. The seminary placement director informed me that campus churches rarely call someone straight out of the seminary.

When Call Day arrived, I doubted that whatever call I received could interest me as much as campus ministry. But when I opened the call documents, a miracle took place. Instantly I could sense a new desire to do this unexpected work that the Lord had chosen for me. It was just like God had turned off a faucet marked 'campus ministry' and had turned on another faucet labeled 'starting a church from scratch in Lafayette, Indiana.' I know now that the Lord makes clear to all who await the church's call that it is also his call. And he can be trusted, for "in all things God works for the good of those who love him" (Rom. 8:28).

No matter where God may send you, it is important to realize that God has a *global* plan. I (Phil) had blindly accepted what some call "The Comfortable Doctrine" of missions. It claims that if people in India or Africa want to hear about Christ, they need only seek out the Christians in their country. For the first four years of my ministry I believed this. The problem was, I was failing to see the world as God sees it and failing to love the world as God loves it. I needed to learn some facts.

Approximately 5.6 billion people populate the earth, 4.3 billion without saving faith in Christ. Some experts estimate that 1.2 billion are completely unevangelized, with virtually no Christians living among them. At least another billion are cut off from any effective Christian witness by geography, language, culture, and governments hostile towards the Gospel. (See David B. Barrett, "Annual Statistical Table on Global Mission: 1993," *International Bulletin of Missionary Research,* vol. 17, no. 1, 22-23.)

Christ said, "Go and make disciples of all nations" (Matt. 28:19). The word translated as "nations" means "people who share an ethnic heritage." The church's target, therefore, is not simply the 200 or so nations of the world, but the total sum of all cultural groups. Some anthropologists list that number at 22,000. And the church has been successfully planted among only 10,000. Thus, 2.2 billion people in 12,000 cultures will be reached only by cross-cultural mission work. They will not come to us, because the cultural gap is too wide. The church will have to build bridges to them—that is, send missionaries.

Finding a You-Sized Role

Accurate, compelling statistics such as these blew away the smoke screen of the Comfortable Doctrine so that I could see the world as God sees it. Now that I could not hide, did I throw up my hands in despair and give up? Surprisingly, no. Instead, I simply decided to *do* the little I could. God's great global goal can be attained by the church if each individual Christian will simply take a one-person-sized part of the whole job. What a relief!

I encourage you to design for yourself a one-person-sized role. First, include a prayer component. With the help of mission publications, you can become a "prayer missionary," supporting ministry in any country of the world. Second, include mission education. Learn about the church's work throughout the world. Share with other Christians the challenges and joys of world evangelism. Third, get involved in cross-cultural ministry right where you are. U.S. campuses host over 400,000 foreign students every year. What if some of them were to return home as Christians? Also, legions of refugees are seeking to start life all over. You and others in your church can provide them a new life and lead them to eternal life in Christ.

By playing your one-person-sized role in God's global mission, your life and ministry will be more rewarding and meaningful than ever before. There is another sweet by-product: freedom from guilt. When I believed the Comfortable Doctrine, I had not actually been very comfortable; my conscience had often felt little pricks of guilt, telling me, "Shouldn't you be doing *something*?" Once I learned the truth, I felt free from guilt about the task of evangelizing *all* nations. Finally I was contributing my me-sized share to fulfilling the Great Commission. That was all God expected of me, and it was enough.

I encourage you to see that world missions can play an important role in your life right now as well as in your future church career. All the church professions described in this book have their counterparts in cross-cultural settings where Christian workers are scarce. The need for missionaries is urgent. In order to place two missionaries among the 2.2 billion people in 12,000 target groups, the Christian church needs to increase its missionary force by over 600,000 people. Dollars will help, but what we need more than anything is people willing to witness and exercise their spiritual gifts in another culture.

As you ponder where in the world God will send you,

be sure to remain open to cross-cultural (even overseas) service. Why? Following his resurrection, Jesus' primary topic was "Go to all the nations!" Earlier, establishing his kingdom of grace throughout the world had come first. But after he had broken the chains of sin, death, and the devil for all people for all time, the next thing on his mind was getting the word to the nations: "As the Father has sent me, I am sending you" (John 20:21).

The Hardest Job in the World

Serving in a foreign culture has been called the hardest job in the world. Everyone who does so suffers temporarily from culture shock, the painful reaction to adjusting to a setting completely different from your own. Yet the person with missionary potential recovers from it and eventually grows to appreciate the culture and love the people in it.

Do you have this gift? The best way to find out is to spend time with people of an ethnic background other than your own. If you have even a small interest in cross-cultural ministry, try to experience a foreign culture prior to graduation from college or seminary. Such opportunities may exist right in your own backyard. Can you eventually feel comfortable with folks of another culture? Can you develop friendships in spite of your differences? If so, you probably could be a missionary. And don't be afraid of any future language barriers. You will be amazed how quickly you pick up the language when you live in a place where you have to speak it.

No one has ever had to cross a wider cultural chasm than Jesus did. No one of us has ever had to suffer like he did. No one of us would ever have been saved if this cross-cultural worker had not crossed the chasm between the worlds to die on the cross in our place. Thus he earned the right to charge us with the task of going to all the peoples to make them his disciples.

Since our God is a missionary God, follow his example. As you ponder a church career and aspire to it, may God the Holy Spirit guide you to see the you-sized role that he has selected for you to play in the unparalleled drama of world evangelization. Whether you remain a lay person or become a church worker, whether you serve locally or overseas, may our Lord cause you to play your role well, until you hear him call, "Well done, good and faithful servant!" (Matt. 25:21).

Consider This

1. List all the cross-cultural experiences you have had in your life. Include even the small things. Do you see any pattern? Could this possibly indicate where God might someday have you concentrate your ministry concern?

2. What are the chances that you could become a cross-cultural worker in your own country? How might you prepare for this likelihood?

3. Think of someone you know who follows another religion: Islam, Buddhism, New Age, atheism, etc. What are some things that you would need to learn or experience in order to be moderately effective at sharing Christ with that person? How might you gain such training?

4. How can you promote a world mission attitude in your local church?

5. Make a list of all the reasons why perhaps you should *not* consider ministering cross-culturally. Make another list of all the reasons why you should. Pray your way through the two lists, asking for the Lord's direction. Seek the advice of other believers. See the catalog in Part 2 for further details about missionary careers.

Part 2
CATALOG

===

Christian Social Worker

Through Christian counseling and other social services that seek to improve social conditions for those in need, helps clients achieve a greater measure of good health and well being and the ability to become productive members of society.

Qualifications

Spiritual qualifications
- Faith in the triune God
- Spiritual maturity
- Self-discipline and self-control
- A sense of servanthood
- A heart of love for all people
- Patience

Personality traits
- Responsible
- Committed to service
- Self-regulating
- Able to identify and use resources
- Autonomous
- Friendly
- A good listener
- Accepting of differences

Education

A Bachelor of Science degree in social work from an accredited institution, with 500 hours of field work in the junior and senior years. For a lifetime career, consider earning a Masters of Social Work degree.

Lutheran social workers take extra

To the people I was visiting I was a person, not just a social worker doing my job. Results in my work with AIDS patients cannot always be seen within the people I visited. I hope and pray that somehow I may have bettered their lives. I do know that they have bettered my life. "Go out and make disciples," "forgive sins," and "preach the Gospel to the ends of the earth" always ran through my head as I talked with these people.

course work in theology and social science in order to be eligible for a call through the Lutheran Church—Missouri Synod to a congregation or agency in the LCMS.

In addition: Optional membership in the Academy of Certified Baccalaureate Social Workers (for graduates from an accredited program) shows national professional recognition from peers and employees and assists in meeting state regulations primarily designed to protect the public. There is also a professional membership possible with the National Association of Christians in Social Work.

Variety of Christian Social Workers

Social workers provide services in areas such as these:
- Hospitals
- Mental health
- Corrections
- Family service agencies
- Nursing homes
- Health care
- Schools
- Child welfare
- Public welfare
- Developmentally challenged
- Home care
- Community service
- Drug abuse
- Alcohol abuse

Brief History

Since the days of the early church, ministry to people has included services of compassion toward human beings in physical, mental, and spiritual need. Jesus himself, by his example of healing the deaf, mute, blind, and lame, showed the Christian church that he was concerned not only for spiritual needs but the needs of the whole person. The LCMS is also involved in a ministry of compassion toward humans in need.

Social work as we know it today actually began at the turn of the 20th century in order to provide social services to those exploited in the work force, the poor, children of neglect and abuse, women seeking rights, the homeless, and others.

Christian Teacher

Teaches students a variety of subjects while applying a Christian perspective, develops a caring and loving community in the classroom, and instructs students through God's Word to grow in spiritual wisdom and faith.

Qualifications

Spiritual qualifications
- A vibrant faith in the triune God
- Knowledge of the Bible and doctrine
- A strong worship and devotional life
- Ability and eagerness to teach
- Self-discipline and self-control
- A heart of love for children
- Gentleness, kindness, patience

Personality traits
- Emotionally stable
- A sense of humor
- Able to get along with others
- Persevering
- Humble
- Understanding

Primary understandings
- The primary objective of teaching is learning
- Christian education centers all subjects around God's Word
- The Christian teacher is a role model of faith and life

Education

A Bachelor of Science or Arts degree in teacher education, which includes field work experiences and student teaching under the direction of an experienced teacher. Students will select to be licensed in a particular level: early childhood, kindergarten, elementary, middle school, secondary,

There is no greater joy for me than to watch students learn something new. My favorite time to teach is when they are hungering to know more. I enjoy teaching religion more than any other subject. Of all the subjects that are taught, none is more important than teaching the saving Gospel of Jesus Christ.

or special education. In addition, teachers are certified or licensed in areas such as history, science, math, music, physical education, art, and coaching.

Varieties of Service

Classroom Teacher
In most grade schools, teachers are responsible for a variety of subjects. Specialties may include preschool and special education. Most high schools assign teachers specific subjects—usually your undergraduate major or minor.

Principals and Superintendents
Teachers who become principals or superintendents are responsible also for administering the school's overall operation.

Part-Time Teachers
Some teachers find they enjoy teaching part-time or on a substitute basis while pursuing another career interest.

Missionaries
These teachers, in domestic multicultural and overseas settings, may prepare congregational members to teach others, teach missionary children, or teach English as a second language.

Brief History

The function of teaching the next generation has been carried on since Adam and Eve. Joseph (1,700 years B.C.) learned from teachers in Egypt. Eli taught Samuel (1,000 years B.C.). By the time of Christ, the local rabbi seems to have carried out this function among God's people. The role and function of a believer who taught reading, writing, etc., as well as God's Word to children was well in place by the time of the famous Christian teacher Origen (about 200 years after Christ).

At the time of the Reformation, certain groups had attempted to establish schools apart from the church. Luther, however, wrote, "Where the Holy Scripture does not rule I certainly advise no one to send his child. ... I greatly fear that schools for higher learning are wide gates to hell if they do not diligently teach the Holy Scriptures and impress them on the young folk."

The Lutheran Church—Missouri Synod has continued to provide Christian education within its communities of ministry. Today there are over 2,100 Lutheran childhood centers, elementary schools, high schools, colleges, universities, and seminaries in North America.

Church Musician

In the spirit of service to God and his people, serves the church by leading congregational members in the music of worship. Also often assists with worship planning.

Full-time placement in church music more easily comes to those who possess strong music abilities as well as a broad range of church work skills. Some have begun as part-time musicians and later became full-time Directors of Parish Music. Many now serve in larger congregations and study to earn advanced degrees in music. Parish musicians may also teach music or perform professionally.

Qualifications

Spiritual qualifications
- Faith in the triune God
- A joy for worship
- A strong devotional life
- A sense of God's presence in one's life
- Patience
- Self-discipline and self-control
- A sense of servanthood
- A sense of vocation directed to congregational service

Personality traits
- Emotionally stable
- Persevering
- Able to work with others
- Able to work independently to improve musical skills

Musical prerequisites for enrollment
- Choral experience
- Good keyboard talent, usually at the piano (having progressed to, e.g., the study of Bach's two-part inventions or similar material)

All my life I have had a love for music and a desire to serve my Lord. Striving to become a successful musician, I searched for a quality undergraduate education and discovered the Director of Parish Music Program. Both my love for music, and my love for ministry to God's people were filled in this one career. One of the greatest joys for me is to lead amateur singers to a higher level of musical quality. Training the choirs to create music that sounds better than they ever thought possible is a great thrill.

Education

A Bachelor of Arts degree, majoring in music, plus field work experience. The training provides the following:

- Performance skills
- Training in teaching others how to perform music
- Basic competence in directing a choir
- Ability to arrange choral, instrumental, or organ music as required in the congregational setting
- Knowledge and experience in the lectionary and church year as applied to worship planning

Although church music will be the principle field of study, training in an additional church work field increases one's opportunity to serve as church musician. Therefore, students are encouraged also to elect an academic minor or concentration (where available) in another church field:

- Parish education
- Christian teacher
- Director of Christian education
- Early childhood
- Director of Christian outreach
- Evangelism
- Ministry to the aging

Brief History

People of God throughout Old and New Testament times have been praising and worshiping God through singing and playing instruments. Music has always been an important element in the worship life of the church.

In the Lutheran church, music is to proclaim the Word of God and to confess one's faith in Jesus Christ. During the Reformation, Luther compared the importance of music to theology. He called it "a living voice of the Gospel, a gift of God to be used in all its fullness in Christian praise and prayer."

Many musicians in the church today work as full-time parish staffers. Others work as part-time parish music directors, serving as organists and choir directors while employed full-time in other careers.

Because of rising expectations in congregations for better music, a program specifically designed to train professional musicians (Director of Parish Music) was established at some colleges of the LCMS in the early 1970s.

Deaconess

As a spiritual caregiver, assists and supports the ministry of the pastoral office through service and leadership in a congregation, specialized Lutheran agency, or mission field.

The specific service provided by a deaconess will depend upon her training and the congregation or agency in which she works.

Qualifications

Spiritual qualifications
- A mature faith
- A love of studying and teaching God's Word
- A servant attitude and humility
- A caring and sensitive attitude
- A heart of love for all people

Personality traits
- A compassionate leader
- Able to communicate with many age groups
- Flexible
- Able to work independently and with co-workers
- A good listener

Education

The undergraduate degree at Concordia University, River Forest, Illinois, includes a theology major, specialized deaconess courses, 150 hours of field work, and a year of internship. Students may choose specialized studies from these areas:

- Social work
- Psychology
- Sociology
- Church music
- Counseling
- Youth ministry
- Education
- Deaf ministry
- Gerontology
- Foreign language or Greek

After considering other careers in which I couldn't really share my faith, I chose this, because there are so many ways to serve God in deaconess work. The emphasis on caring for people's spiritual needs is wonderful; I bring God's comfort to hurting people.

Students with a degree may combine deaconess education with a Master of Arts in Religion, Psychology, or Human Services.

Variety of Deaconesses

Parish Deaconess

Half of all deaconesses work in a parish. They assist the pastor in caring for people's spiritual needs. This includes visiting the sick and hospitalized, the homebound, prospective members, and anyone with special needs. The deaconess comforts the grieving, teaches Bible classes and confirmation classes, and works with special groups such as women, youth, singles, etc.

Institutional Chaplaincy

Hospitals utilize deaconesses to provide spiritual care to patients and families. Hospitals often require Clinical Pastoral Education in addition to deaconess training.

Homes for the developmentally disabled and homes for the aged call deaconesses to provide spiritual care for residents. This is done through Bible classes and personal visits.

Professional Counselor

A deaconess with a Master's degree in social work or psychology may serve in a Lutheran social service agency.

Missionary

The LCMS Board for Mission Services places deaconesses and interns in mission work both in the United States and overseas. Lutheran Bible Translators also sends deaconesses into missions.

Brief History

Phoebe (Rom. 16:1-2) is considered to be the first deaconess of the Christian church. During the church's first four centuries, deaconess responsibilities included teaching and giving spiritual care to women and children, serving the physical needs of the imprisoned and impoverished, mediating between the bishop and women, overseeing the conduct of women in worship, and assisting in baptisms of women.

Within the Lutheran church, the office of the deaconess began in 1836. Training within the Lutheran Church—Missouri Synod began in 1919 by the Lutheran Deaconess Association. The only deaconess program of the LCMS is now at Concordia University, River Forest, Illinois, and was established in 1980.

Director of Christian Education

Teaches the faith, directs educational ministries, and nurtures God's people of all ages in Christian discipleship within a congregation.

Specific duties of the DCE may include the following:
- Ascertaining the educational needs of the congregation
- Setting goals and objectives
- Administering the church's Christian education program
- Motivating and training volunteers for Christian service

Qualifications

Spiritual qualifications
- A vibrant faith in the triune God
- Knowledge of the Bible and doctrine
- A strong worship and devotional life
- Self-discipline and self-control
- A heart of love for people
- A sense of servanthood
- Forgiveness, gentleness, kindness
- An ability to teach

Personality traits
- A good listener
- Understanding
- Skillful in leadership and creative problem-solving
- Energetic
- Socially skilled
- Able to work with others, professional and lay

Education
A Bachelors degree from a college with a DCE program, which includes an additional year of internship. The first two years of the five-year program focus on general education courses. Two of the last three years concentrate on the future work

As Lutheran teachers teach the faith in the classroom setting, the DCE teaches the faith in a congregational setting. As a parish educator, I specifically attempt to focus the lives of young people and adults on their faith in Jesus Christ. Connecting life situations to faith in the Savior helps them to ultimately understand their role in the body of Christ.

of the DCE, plus courses for the student's selected area of specialization, which includes these options:

- Music
- Worship
- Youth ministry
- Family ministry
- Outdoor ministry
- Counseling
- Evangelism
- Administration

Variety of Directors of Christian Education

Congregational

- Lutheran elementary school teachers
- Directors of a parish's Christian education
- Directors of specific areas of congregational ministry such as evangelism, music, youth, family, counseling, group dynamics, etc.

Outdoor Ministry Directors

- Camp administrative/executive director
- Program director

Missionaries

- At-home/domestic missionary
- Overseas missionary

Brief History

In the early church, teachers of the faith were called catechists. They were nurturers who taught believers of all ages how to grow in their faith and live their lives as children of grace.

During the early years of the Lutheran Church—Missouri Synod, some parochial teachers not only taught day school but also directed new parish educational programs such as the Sunday school. Their primary focus was the religious training of a congregation's youth.

Some form of the title "Education Director" began to be utilized around 1916. As responsibilities for the director increased with the development of weekday school and vacation church school programs, so did the need for full-time directors. In 1959 the LCMS officially recognized the role of the Director of Christian Education.

Director of Christian Outreach

Oversees and trains members to do personal witnessing, to assimilate new members, and to conduct multicultural outreach.

Parish evangelism responsibilities of the DCO:
- Develops prayer support for the church's outreach
- Stimulates lay involvement in evangelism
- Designs new and innovative strategies to bring Christ's message to the unchurched
- Discovers the unchurched in the community and leads them to hear Christ's invitation to them
- Teaches members to become more comfortable and effective in sharing Christ
- Is the voice of the unchurched to the congregation, informing church members of the needs of the community and urging them to take appropriate actions of Christian service and witness
- Develops strategies to assimilate new members
- Ministers to inactive church members

Qualifications

Spiritual qualifications
- A vibrant faith in Christ
- Knowledge of the Bible and doctrine
- A strong worship and devotional life
- A deep concern for those without faith in Christ
- An eagerness to witness
- Patience
- An ability to listen to, understand, and love non-Christians

[Note: The spiritual gift of evangelist is not a requirement. Some DCOs have it; some do not.]

Personality traits
- Emotionally stable
- Persevering
- Able to get along with others

Many people today feel that the church has become stagnant, stuffy, and impersonal. Therefore, they assume that God has become irrelevant. I want to show them otherwise.

- Able to speak effectively in public
- Skillful in administration

Education

A Bachelors degree from a college with a DCO program, which includes an additional year of internship. Those who already have a degree in another field usually need two years plus internship. Study courses include the following:
- Evangelism and missions
- Bible and doctrine
- Church history
- Worship
- Administration

Variety of Directors of Christian Outreach

Specialized areas of ministry may include the following:
- Youth work
- Music
- Drama
- Family ministries
- Worship
- Multicultural outreach
- Media ministry
- Service to more than one congregation
- Consultant for neighboring congregations
- Regional or national evangelism committees
- Team of cross-cultural missionaries

Brief History

Among the ministry roles in the early church is that of the evangelist (Acts 21:8; Eph. 4:11; and 2 Tim. 4:5). Evangelists were especially gifted at sharing the Gospel with unbelievers in such a manner that the Holy Spirit could work faith in their hearts. Some were traveling Christians whose primary work was to proclaim the Good News in new areas.

In the second half of the 20th century, many clergy found themselves unable to be effective evangelists due to other heavy responsibilities and lack of training. Since 1979, lay people, eager to share their faith, have been trained in the Director of Christian Outreach program at Concordia College, St. Paul, Minnesota.

Lay Minister

Carries out a variety of ministries within a parish and under the supervision of a pastor. The position is open to men and women.

Qualifications

Spiritual qualifications
- A vibrant faith in the triune God
- Knowledge of the Bible and doctrine
- A strong worship and devotional life
- Self-discipline and self-control
- Patience
- A heart of love for people

Personality traits
- Emotionally stable
- Able to get along with others
- Persevering

Ministry desires
- To understand and articulate the mission of the church
- To serve as a team player
- To follow the guidance and direction of pastoral leadership
- To learn to identify, guide, and use the gifts and talents of lay people
- To become a Christian role model and to guide especially the leaders of the congregation to do so also

Education

A Bachelor of Arts degree with a theology major from a college with a Lay Minister program. Some available minors:
- Youth ministry
- Church administration
- Teaching

After serving actively as a lay leader in my congregation for a number of years, I realized just how much more my pastor could do if he were provided quality assistance. Once I received my professional training, I was called as his assistant. Not all will be fortunate enough to be supported and called by their home congregation, but pastors are searching for professionals to assist them in leading a congregation in discipleship.

- Older adults ministry
- Social ministry and visitation
- Evangelism
- Deaf ministry

Varieties of Service

Parish Lay Minister
These ministers serve larger congregations in specialized areas as a pastoral assistant.

Deacon
Male lay ministers serve small parishes as deacons, providing a Word-and-Sacrament ministry under the direct supervision of an area ordained pastor.

Mission Developer
These lay ministers develop and maintain "start-up" mission congregations.

Part-time Lay Minister
Some lay ministers serve more than one parish or simultaneously work at a secular career to earn a living.

Other Avenues of Service
Institutional chaplains, teachers, executives, staff at colleges and district offices, etc. Those who specialize in inner-city and cross-cultural ministry serve in a variety of leadership roles.

Brief History

Ever since Stephen and the early church (see Acts 6:1-7), faithful and dedicated lay people have assisted in the ministry and mission of the church. Beginning in 1946, Rev. Oscar E. Feucht, considered to be the founding father of the Lay Ministry program in the Lutheran Church—Missouri Synod, began encouraging the ongoing education of adult lay people in congregations. Finally, in 1961, the Lutheran Lay Training Institute become a reality, first housed at Concordia College, Milwaukee (now in Mequon), Wisconsin.

A colloquy extension program for lay ministry was developed in 1970. This program consisted of correspondence and summer courses. In 1992 this program developed into a Theological Education by Extension model (TEE) to allow students to take courses within designated geographical regions instead of moving to a college campus for course-work training.

Missionary

Displays Christ's love by word and deed in a culture or environment different from their own, sharing the Gospel with those who have not heard it.

Qualifications

Spiritual qualifications
- A vibrant faith in the triune God
- Knowledge of the Bible and doctrine
- A strong worship and devotional life
- The ability and eagerness to witness
- Self-discipline and self-control
- Patience
- A heart of love for people

Personality traits
- Emotionally stable
- Adaptable to cultures
- Good-natured
- Able to get along with others
- Able to endure hardship
- Persevering
- Humble

Education
Training at a college with a program in missions. Nonclergy missionaries with a Bachelors degree should spend at least one additional school year studying courses such as these:
- Bible
- Christian doctrine
- Worship
- Church history in general
- History and theology of missions
- Mission principles and strategies
- World religions

At first, it didn't seem right to be a missionary in a modern city. But under the veneer of cosmopolitan amusements I found great personal uncertainty, fear of evil spirits, and deep sorrow instilled by Buddhist philosophy. The city is where God wants me and many other missionaries to be.

- Cultural anthropology
- Intercultural communication
- Personal witnessing/evangelism
- Language acquisition
- Missionary internship experiences

Variety of Missionaries

Evangelistic missionaries often are pastors, teachers, deaconesses, DCEs, DCOs, etc. Their main tasks are as follows:
- Lead people to Christ
- Equip people for Christian service and outreach
- Plant new congregations
- Establish a locally directed national church

Other roles:
- Bible translator
- Evangelist
- Bible and tract distributor
- Christian bookstore operator

Support missionaries are employed by a mission board to enhance the work of evangelistic missionaries. Examples:
- Teachers for missionary children
- Medical missionaries
- Construction experts
- Missionary pilots
- Agricultural experts
- Mechanics and repairmen
- Business managers
- Literacy workers

Brief History

Missionaries have been an essential part of the church's ministry since the days of Christ. The word *missionary,* like *apostle,* means "one who is sent." New Testament missionaries included the 12 apostles, Paul, Timothy, Luke, Priscilla, and Aquila. Because of missionaries through the centuries, the Good News has reached many, many people.

A century ago, missionaries traveled to foreign lands. Today, God is bringing hundreds of unreached people groups to our own country. Therefore, a missionary is any Christian involved in cross-cultural ministry anywhere, even next door.

Parish Worker

Serves as a Christian business secretary or parish office manager who assists the pastor in the mission of the congregation.

Specific duties may include these:
- Serving as an administrative assistant
- Assisting committees and volunteer organizations
- Serving as secretary on church boards
- Keeping official church records
- Coordinating facilities usage
- Organizing and supervising volunteer office assistance
- Printing church publications
- Typing
- Receiving visitors and telephone contacts
- Organizing all church mailings

Qualifications

Spiritual qualifications
- Faith in the triune God
- A strong worship and devotional life
- Self-discipline and self-control
- A heart of love for people
- Patience

Personality traits
- Flexible
- Adaptable
- Friendly and hospitable
- Able to greet/serve strangers
- Willing to accept and/or create change

What Two Parish Workers Say

When I was called as parish worker, I began to discover new ministry and service opportunities which I had never thought of before. The ministry team is very supportive of my role as office manager, and they allow me to administrate the office without interference. The guidance and supervision of the administrative pastor has helped me to discover gifts and skills that enhance my ministry role.

Office management is very pleasing work, but leading the evangelism and visitation teams is most satisfying. Visiting is one of my primary gifts. Members confined to their homes need to talk to someone. I really enjoy conversing with those who have so many years of spiritual wisdom to share. Visiting potential members in the community is also an exciting challenge. Now I am leading an evangelism ministry in our congregation.

Education

The parish worker program of the LCMS is an adaptation of the business secretarial program. Those who complete the two-year program receive an Associate in Applied Science degree. Additional responsibilities often include Christian education and music.

Varieties of Service

The parish worker may be involved in other aspects of church ministry. Some may serve the church in specialized areas of ministry such as these:
- Music
- Evangelism
- Visitation
- Education
- Youth

Brief History

The parish worker program of the Lutheran Church—Missouri Synod was developed in the early 1930s by Prof. G. A. Kuhlmann at St. John's College, Winfield, Kansas. As originally designed, the program was developed as a two-year degree at the collegiate level to educate and train women to serve principally as church secretaries and church office managers. They also took some very basic courses in education and music so they could assist in the parochial school programs. The purpose of the program was to supply assistants who were committed to the church and who had education and training for office management.

In the late 1950s the parish worker program was revised to include training in parish music and part-time Christian education. Today, the program has basically remained the same with some revisions to meet the needs of contemporary society.

When St. John's College closed its doors in 1985, the program was moved first to Concordia College in Milwaukee, Wisconsin, then to Concordia College, Bronxville, New York, where it remains today.

Although the parish worker program has been a church professional program designed to prepare women, it has never been limited specifically to women.

Pastor

Proclaims and teaches the Word of God, administers the Sacraments, announces the forgiveness of sins, counsels and leads people to grow in Christian faith and life.

Responsibilities include the following:
- Performing marriages and funerals
- Teaching
- Visiting the sick and homebound
- Spiritual counseling
- Designing, guiding, and leading worship,
  personal witnessing, and
  the mission of the congregation

Qualifications

Spiritual qualifications
- A vibrant faith in the triune God
- A heart of love for people
- Knowledge of the Bible and doctrine
- A strong worship and devotional life
- The ability and eagerness to witness
- The ability to teach
- Self-discipline, self-control, and patience

Personality traits
- Emotionally stable
- Persevering
- Responsible
- Humble, yet a leader
- Able to identify and use resources
- Socially skilled

Education

Beyond a Bachelors degree, a Master of Divinity degree, which includes three years of classroom study (with field education) plus a year of internship under the direction of a

As a parish pastor, I am truly blessed with the wonderful opportunity to spiritually serve God's people from the day they are born to the day they are called to their heavenly home. Bringing the healing message of the Gospel to people is a noble and honorable task.

60

parish pastor. Includes learning and using the original languages of Scripture: Hebrew and Greek.

Variety of Pastors

Parish pastors serve one congregation.

Senior/administrative pastors oversee a congregation's entire professional team.

Associate/assistant pastors, serving in designated areas, complement the work of the senior pastor.

Multiple-parish pastors serve two or more parishes at the same time; sometimes called "circuit riders."

Visitation pastors serve and visit the homebound, the sick, the elderly, and the physically challenged.

Church planters begin new congregations and assist newly formed congregations to grow from the ground up.

Bi-vocational pastors hold two jobs, secular and congregational.

Outside the local parish, pastors may serve in the following roles:
- Chaplains at institutions or in the military
- Christian counselors (with an advanced degree)
- Church consultants (following many years of experience)
- Cross-cultural pastors (domestic and overseas)

Specialized areas of ministry include the following:
- Family/youth/elderly
- Differently abled
- Education/evangelism/stewardship
- Urban/rural
- Cross-cultural
- Human care ministry

Brief History

The New Testament portrays the pastor as an undershepherd, called to serve a local flock in the stead of Jesus, the Great Shepherd. Words synonymous with the word *pastor* in the New Testament are *bishop, elder,* and *overseer.* Each of these refers to the office of the public ministry, the pastor. Among the first Christian pastors were Timothy and Titus, appointed by God through the apostle Paul to serve in Ephesus and Crete. Titus was also instructed to appoint pastors for other towns. Through the centuries God has continued to care for his church through faithful pastors.

Appendix 1
Resource List

Bickel, Philip M. *Joy to the World: An Introduction to Christian Missions.* St. Louis: Concordia Publishing House, 1990. An introduction to mission work written especially for Lutherans.

Bickel, Philip M., and Robert L. Nordlie. *The Goal of the Gospel: God's Purpose in Saving You.* St. Louis: Concordia Publishing House, 1992. Learn how Christ's saving work equips you for a life of obedience, mission, and glorifying God.

Bolles, Richard B. *What Color Is Your Parachute? 1993: A Practical Manual for Job Hunters and Career Changers.* Berkeley: Ten Speed Press, 1992. A major resource on career selection. The graphics alone are worth the price of the book.

Diehl, William E. *Thank God, It's Monday.* Philadelphia: Fortress Press, 1982. Learn about the biblical view of all careers as forms of ministry.

Giertz, Bo Harald. *The Hammer of God: A Novel about the Cure of Souls.* Translated by Clifford A. Nelson. Minneapolis: Augsburg, 1973. A theological novel that portrays what it means to share God's Law and Gospel with troubled individuals.

Lindvall, Michael L. *The Good News from North Haven: A Year in the Life of a Small Town.* New York: Doubleday, 1991. A young pastor reflects with sensitivity and humor on his early ministry in a small town parish.

Little, Paul E. *Affirming the Will of God.* Downers Grove, Ill: InterVarsity Press, 1971. A little booklet packed with loads of clear, practical advice about how to determine and affirm God's will for your life.

Miller, Arthur F., and Ralph T. Mattson. *The Truth about You.* Berkeley: Ten Speed Press, 1989. Presents the concept of motivated abilities: the things you do best and love to do.

Moorman, Donald. *Harvest Waiting.* St. Louis: Concordia Publishing House, 1993. A history of multiculturalism in America with suggestions on how to reach out to the peoples of the world whom God has brought to your neighborhood.

Westermeyer, Paul. *The Church Musician.* Harper & Row, 1988. A comprehensive handbook for choir directors, organists, song leaders, and others in the ministry of music.

Educational Institutions of
The Lutheran Church—Missouri Synod
and Their Programs for Full-Time Church Work

Some of the programs listed are certified and some are simply majors. This can make a difference in graduate school and in one's listing in the synodical roster. Check with the appropriate institution for further information.

For school addresses, see next page	ANN ARBOR	AUSTIN	BRONXVILLE	FORT WAYNE	IRVINE	MEQUON	PORTLAND	RIVER FOREST	SAINT LOUIS	SAINT PAUL	SELMA	SEWARD
Christian Social Worker (pre-social work)			X		X	o	X	X				
Christian Teacher	X	X	X		X	X	X	X		X	X	X
Church Musician		X	X			X	X	X		X		X
Deaconess (pre-deaconess)			o					X				
Dir. of Christian Ed.					X		X	X		X		X
Dir. of Chr. Outreach (cross-cultural)										X / o		
Lay Minister (ethnic/Hispanic)			o			X						
Parish Worker			X									
Pastor—seminary (pre-seminary)	o	o	o	X	o	o	o	o	X	o	o	o

Educational Institutions
of the LCMS

Concordia College
4090 Geddes Rd.
Ann Arbor, MI 48105
School: 313/995-7300
Admission: 1-800/253-0680

Concordia College
2811 NE Holman St.
Portland, OR 97211
School: 503/288-9371
Admission: 503/280-8501
                    1-800/321-9371

Concordia Lutheran College
of Texas
3400 North Interstate 35
Austin, TX 78705
School: 512/452-7661
                    1-800/285-4CLC
Admission: 512/452-7661

Concordia University
7400 Augusta St.
River Forest, IL 60305-1499
School: 708/771-8300
Admission: 708/209-3100
                    1-800/285-2668

Concordia College
171 White Plains Rd.
Bronxville, NY 10708-1923
School: 914/337-9300
Admission: 914/337-9300 x2571
                    1-800/973-2655

Concordia Seminary
801 De Mun Ave.
St. Louis, MO 63105
School: 314/721-5934

Concordia Theological Seminary
6600 N. Clinton St.
Fort Wayne, IN 46825-4996
School: 219/481-2100

Concordia College
275 N. Syndicate St.
St. Paul, MN 55104
School: 612/641-8278
Admission: 612/641-8230

Concordia University
1530 Concordia West
Irvine, CA 92715-3299
School: 714/854-8002
Admission:: 714/854-8002 x106
                    1-800/229-1200

Concordia College
1804 Green St.
Selma, AL 36701
School: 205/874-5700
Admission: 205/874-5715

Concordia University Wisconsin
12800 N. Lake Shore Dr.
Mequon, WI 53092
School: 414/243-5700
Admission: 414/243-4300

Concordia College
800 N. Columbia Ave.
Seward, NE 68434
School: 402/643-3651
Admission: 402/643-7233

CPSIA information can be obtained
at www.ICGtesting.com
Printed in the USA
JSHW020422120723
44434JS00002B/73